D1636833

the RIGHT STORY

A BRIEF GUIDE
to CHANGING *the* WORLD

BERNADETTE JIWA

"It is stories—both real and fictional—that can captivate hearts, change minds, and, in the most powerful examples, spur action."

—VANESSA DIFFENBAUGH

Published in Australia by Perceptive Press.
www.thestoryoftelling.com

National Library of Australia Publication Data
available via www.nla.gov.au

ISBN: 978-0-9944328-2-7

Printed in the United States of America

Cover & Book Design: Reese Spykerman
Interior Layout: Kelly Exeter

10 9 8 7 6 5 4 3 2 1

First Edition

*For Reese, whose work is a gift that changes how
we see the world.*

CONTENTS

INTRODUCTION

"The real difference between us and chimpanzees is the mysterious glue that enables millions of humans to cooperate effectively. This mysterious glue is made of stories, not genes."

—YUVAL NOAH HARARI

Time was running out for the archaeologists at Wood Quay. The bulldozers moved in. Construction crews had been on site for months, ready and waiting to dig foundations for the planned office development on the site, where a Viking settlement had once stood, a thousand years before. That Viking village became the city of Dublin—the capital of Ireland, where I was born and raised.

*

Stories are how
we change things.
We can't make
progress without
them.

*

Despite public disquiet, plans had been agreed and set in motion to build new council offices on the land acquired by Dublin Corporation between 1950 and 1975. Four high-rise granite and glass buildings would rise up next to the historic Christ Church Cathedral. But those plans stalled when early excavation work uncovered a 'mediaeval time capsule' preserved in the anaerobic soil. This record of early urban life in Viking Dublin was an internationally significant archaeological find.

As consultant archaeologist Linzi Simpson reported, what emerged was 'layer upon layer of urban living from the Viking period and beyond. The remains were astonishing: complete foundations of wattle-and-daub houses; interior hearths and benches; workshops; timber pathways and boundary fences; and even latrines and rubbish pits filled with unique artefacts. What remained was the archaeological footprint of many generations who lived in the bustling international port known as Dyflinn, founded in the ninth century.'

Following the discovery, archaeologists from the National Museum of Ireland began working at Wood Quay in 1974. Racing against time, they preserved and catalogued artefacts that would otherwise be buried under tons of concrete and steel, granite and glass. They uncovered the foundations of a hundred Viking houses and thousands of objects—hand-carved wooden vessels, tools, decorative jewellery, a child's leather boot. The excitement about these discoveries was tempered with sadness over the hundreds of other undiscovered treasures that would be lost forever, unless the development was stopped.

I visited Wood Quay on a school excursion at the end of 1977, when I was 10 years old. Hundreds of schoolchildren from all over Ireland came to visit the site that year. Archaeologists, historians and teachers were keen to give as many school groups as possible a glimpse of the ancient Viking settlement before it was too late. We saw the archaeologists painstakingly comb the soil with brushes and trowels, learning how the Vikings changed the way cities like Dublin were built, abandoning the central city square, preferring instead to build their settlement curving around the river—looking towards the river and the sea beyond. We saw fragments of ancient tools and jewellery made from metal and stone, wood and bones, and heard about the Viking rune alphabet and the sagas they told. We looked towards the mouth of the river Liffey where the longships had arrived, and began to understand how our Viking ancestors' humanity and ingenuity had shaped and changed our world.

On 23rd September 1978, 20,000 people marched to protest the development, and to 'Save Wood Quay'. The site was designated a national monument that year. Despite the public outcry, protest marches, media attention and international appeals to preserve our heritage, councillors voted to greenlight the development. Even we children sensed that this development was a bad idea. We couldn't figure out why the people in power didn't lift a finger to stop it. We shook our heads in disbelief over the lack of foresight of the elected officials responsible for planning our city's future.

✳

*We can only create
the future we want
to see by bringing
other people with us
on our journey.*

✳

At the core of our bewilderment, and probably yours too, lies a truth about making change happen. It's hard to persuade people to do things they don't want to do. The gap between the councillors' values and beliefs and those of the protesters was too wide to bridge in the time available. The protesters who tried to save Wood Quay didn't have enough time to build on the story the councillors had been telling themselves over several decades about the need for progress. The right story could have helped them to find common ground and been a bridge towards a compromise.

The archaeologists at Wood Quay worked on the site for a total of ten years. The new office buildings were eventually opened in 1986. Today, 40 years after the Save Wood Quay protests, four soulless office buildings now dominate that corner of the Dublin city skyline, a reminder of how far we have come as a nation and a society, and how much more we still have to learn.

Sometimes bad ideas succeed, and we can't stop them. Sometimes good ideas fail and we can't save them. But we can learn from those failures and improve our chances of success. In the intervening years, I've realised that there is no such thing as a bad idea or a good idea. There is only the wrong story or the right story. The right story is one that is trusted. It is believed because it is told by the right person, for the right reasons, in the right way, at the right time, to the right people. The success or failure of our ideas depends on us telling the right story. We can only do that by being clear about the change we want to create, and why—and then bringing enough of the right people with us on the journey. It's up to us, the changemakers of today and tomorrow, to galvanise those people we hope to bring on the journey with us.

That's what this book is about. It's not just about helping you to change someone's mind. It's about how you can get better at articulating the change you want to create and understanding the people you want to influence, inspire or impact—so you can build upon what they already believe and ultimately shape the future you and they want to see.

WHAT'S THE POINT OF STORIES?

Like my Viking ancestors, we are hardwired to survive. We humans have evolved to assess risks and react to threats. More importantly, we know instinctively that our survival depends on more than any one individual's ability to stay alive. We understand the need to connect and collaborate with each other. We want to bond and belong, so we can work together for the greater good of the tribe. And not only our psychology but our physiology ensures that we do.

The amygdala, part of the emotional centre of the brain, is constantly filtering signals and stimulating a response. It's preparing us to react or respond, to flee when we're threatened or empathise when we're emotionally engaged. Neurotransmitters help us to process positive and negative stimuli and prioritise our responses accordingly. When we sense a threat, our brain is flooded with the neurochemical adrenaline, triggering our fight-or-flight response.

The neurochemical oxytocin has the opposite effect, preparing us to tend and befriend. As Professor Paul Zak and his team discovered, 'oxytocin (the

✳

Stories are the cornerstones of human connection and collaboration, drivers of our thoughts and actions.

✳

neurochemical responsible for empathy and narrative transportation) is synthesized in the human brain when one is trusted and that the molecule motivates reciprocation'. According to Zak, 'Narratives that cause us to pay attention and also involve us emotionally are the stories that move us to action.' It's our very makeup, our physiology, that enables us to empathise and to be persuaded by stories. This physiological connection between head and heart is the reason stories work.

Zak goes on to say, 'Stories that are personal and emotionally compelling engage more of the brain, and thus are better remembered, than simply stating a set of facts.' They also proved that 'when the brain synthesizes oxytocin, people are more trustworthy, generous, charitable, and compassionate.'

When we communicate, if our messages don't get past the amygdala and create an emotional response, we are less likely to influence the people we are trying to reach. That's where stories come in.

Stories are how we change things. We can't make progress without them. Stories help us to imagine a future that does not yet exist. Stories reinforce our beliefs about who we are and who it's possible for us to become. They change how we think, feel and act. The mission to put a man on the moon started with a story. But storytelling has been inspiring people to venture forth and reshape the world since long before John F. Kennedy's speech to congress that inspired NASA's 1960's mission.

Those Viking voyages retold in sagas gave people hope of a brighter future. The pyramids, railways, cars, powered crewed flight, that chair you're sitting on, the page you're turning or the device you're holding—all are the results of people imagining that they could change something for the better. Throughout history, stories of scarcity and abundance changed our perception about what was important and valuable. Stories altered the material value of ideas and objects. Stories changed what we paid for things and what we treasured. The value of everything from tulips to shares, diamonds to real estate, bottled water to Bitcoin, depends on people believing a story. Our internal narratives even change what we believe we are capable of.

All stories then—those we tell and those we believe—are powerful catalysts for change. Stories are the cornerstones of human connection and collaboration drivers of our thoughts and actions. As the history books attest, bearing witness to lives and times of people like Rosa Parks and Adolf Hitler, stories have brought us together and driven us apart. A story can teach us how to love, whom to fear and when to act.

Every societal challenge has been solved by persuading others to act in the interests of the group— to do the right thing for the right reasons. From the day we're born to the day we die, we're figuring out how to persuade people. We are aware that we can't do much of anything alone. We can only create the future we want to see by bringing other people with us on our journey. We understand the importance of gaining enrolment, getting agreement or effecting some kind of change of heart. We turn to stories when we're trying to make our partners understand how we feel or get our children to listen to reason. We rely on them when we want to encourage colleagues or

✳

*It's not just what
we say that helps
people to make up
their minds …
It's everything
we do.*

✳

customers to consider an alternative. Stories help us in situations when we're persuading someone to see things differently.

Whether we're in the living room or the classroom, the boardroom or the parliamentary room, every one of us is in the business of changing minds. But you can't change a mind without winning a heart. Every day, we are repeatedly challenged to tell that right story—one that enables an emotional connection with another person. Poor outcomes or undesired results happen because of a breakdown in trust and communication. Whether in our roles as lovers or leaders, we achieve the right outcome by telling the right story to the right person at the right time. The phrase 'on the same page' aptly describes the shared understanding we need to move forward.

What causes businesses to underperform? Why do some leaders employ short-term thinking? What stops people from quitting bad habits? Why don't communities always collaborate? What causes relationships to break down? And why don't children do as they're told? What's stopping us from telling the right story isn't the soundness of our argument, the brilliance of our logic or the quality of the thing we're selling. It's that we haven't understood how best to communicate in a way that helps others to imagine a future they can't yet see.

You can't build a strong argument with flawed logic. You can't get the right outcome with the wrong objectives. You can't persuade someone without earning their trust. You can't build the right company with the wrong story. If you want to make progress or create positive change you need to understand the worldviews of the people you hope to take with you on that journey.

Good storytellers and great communicators seek to understand before being understood. If we want our ideas to fly, then we must be more intentional about the way we go about sharing our message and telling our story.

In this book I want to help you to think about how you can communicate more purposefully and powerfully when you're trying to influence people and create a change for the better. I want to show you how you can begin to tell the right story.

It's important to stress at the outset that I'm using the term 'story' loosely. The conventional definition of story is a narrative about good vs. evil or the triumph and disaster of a hero on a quest, with a beginning, middle and end. For the purposes of this book I'm taking the liberty of defining story as the way we communicate (both verbally and non-verbally), in an attempt to create a change. In business and in life, the gestures we use, the expressions we make, the emails we send, the announcements we broadcast, the signs we design, the gifts we send, the questions we ask, the products and packaging we make, the prices we charge and standards we set are all integral to how we and our companies are perceived and received. It's not just what we say that helps people to make up their minds about whether to trust what we're asking them to believe or believe in. It's everything we do.

ONE

What is the right story?

*"The world is not made of atoms.
It is made of stories."*
—MURIEL RUYKESER

CHANGE IS A HUMAN ACT

Every day is made up of a series of interactions with other people. If those people are not just passers-by, then we're usually trying to communicate with them on a more than superficial level. We are hoping to get their attention, so we can deepen our relationship or effect change. Our personal happiness, fulfilment,

✳

*Progress depends
on people having
a shared sense of
purpose.*

✳

and success—the harmony of our societies—depend to varying degrees on how well we can connect and communicate with others. Progress depends on people having a shared sense of purpose. Lasting change can't happen without agreement and a consensus that we're on the right path together. There's no escaping the fact that at some point we need to engage with and influence others if we're going to make change happen.

The goal won't always be to get them to change their behaviour. Often we're trying to help people to see the world through a different lens, one that causes them to question their worldviews. Renowned experts in the fields of motivation and persuasion, like B. J. Fogg and Robert Cialdini, have shone a light on some of our flawed thinking in the area of human motivation and influence. Through robust scientific experimentation, they have shown us how we can get better at creating the changes we seek in ourselves and others. Their work demonstrates that when we understand why we think, feel and behave the way we do, we improve our chances of creating the change we all want to see.

Every successful new technology must, as Geoffrey Moore pointed out, cross the chasm in order to make a mark and become widely adopted. In his book *Crossing the Chasm*, Moore explained that the first users of a technology—the early adopters—have different expectations to the majority of users. It's only by understanding and appealing to these differing worldviews that the innovator has the best chance of making the product a success.

From the adoption and eventual ubiquity of the humble supermarket trolley, to the sales of the Harry Potter books in their millions, innovations, products and ideas rely on people believing in, using and sharing them. Change happens because enough people are persuaded to act.

It sometimes seems like change happens in a moment, in that split second when people make a choice about whether to act or not to act. When someone chooses to agree or disagree. To support or walk away. But change is a process. It happens by degrees, over time.

We mistakenly believe that changemaking and persuasion are only about getting someone's attention by creating awareness of an issue or option, and then presenting people with rational arguments that will convince them to make choices we find desirable. But both the science and what we ourselves witness in the world around us prove otherwise. Research in the fields of psychology and behavioural sciences demonstrates that people make irrational decisions all the time. We are not driven only by reason and logic. Emotions also play a big part in how we react, what we decide, and whether we choose to change.

Persuasion is the ability to change a belief or behaviour. We persuade by appealing to reason or understanding. But the process of persuasion is more complex than just presenting the information and expecting people to make an objective judgement or rational choice. One of the mistakes we make when we're attempting to persuade is to only appeal to the thinking person and his rational mind. Messages that resonate deeply connect with people's feelings. Successful ideas appeal to people's hearts not just their

＊

*You can't
change a mind
without winning
a heart.*

＊

heads. We don't just persuade people to act. We move them to act.

We are persuaded when we're empowered to make what we believe is the best choice for us—a choice that at worst, we won't later regret, and that at best enables us to live more contented, productive, fulfilling lives. Effective change engages someone in the act of becoming the kind of person they want to be. Engagement is the act of communicating with conviction and empathy to build trust. We instinctively know from a very young age that our ability to engage is vital to achieving the outcome we want, and yet we are never taught how to do it well. We learn to communicate haphazardly, by example, by mimicking our parents, teachers and role models. For all the time we spend attaining knowledge and honing skills, we devote comparatively little time to understanding how to communicate. Yet it's that ability to empathise and engage, then bring people with us on the journey, that's essential to achieving our individual and collective goals. Because we don't have a reliable communication strategy, we end up being inconsistent at best—saying things we don't mean that spoil our chances of achieving a successful outcome. At worst, we ruin our relationships and fail to get people behind us or our ideas.

Picture the scene. Bob has been working in his current job for over a year. He loves the work, but the salary increase he was promised when he joined the company hasn't materialised. In fact, his boss Mike, has never mentioned it again since the day of Bob's interview. Bob wonders if Mike has forgotten about his promise. He knows there's no way around it; he will have to speak to Mike. Bob also knows the outcome he wants. All he has to do is pick his moment.

Instead of scheduling a time to meet with Mike, Bob decides to casually mention his pay rise as they are both rushing to the car park between meetings on a hectic day. Bad idea. Bob doesn't have time to tell Mike how much he's enjoying the job and how he's looking forward to continuing to make a valuable contribution to the team. Mike doesn't recall the promise he made to Bob a year ago. He senses that there's something more to the request for more money than meets the eye. He feels vulnerable and threatened in that moment. His mind is still partly on dealing with the problems presented at the meeting they've just left. He wonders why Bob can't see that. Mike becomes defensive and says he can't make decisions that affect the budget on a whim like this. Both men are embarrassed—and Bob doesn't achieve the outcome he wanted.

We've all done something similar on occasion: chosen the wrong place or time to have a discussion with our partner, became tongue-tied because we didn't prepare what we wanted to say, failed to get the funding or close the sale we needed because we didn't win the trust of key stakeholders.

Why can't we persuade people even when our ideas are sound or what we're proposing is in their best interests? It turns out that we miss the mark because we don't take the audience's mindset and motivations into account. We don't think beyond getting their attention and delivering the message. We fail to connect with people or get their agreement because we are preoccupied with finding the quickest route to

✳

Change happens because enough people are persuaded to act.

✳

the end result—which is usually to get them to take the action we're proposing. We're mainly focused on *our* motivations, and the way we communicate reflects that. And so, we end up saying and doing the wrong thing at the wrong time.

We become better communicators when we understand three things: what we believe to be true, what we want our audience to know, and what the people we hope to influence are open to hearing at that moment.

We can avoid a situation like the one Bob found himself in by asking five key questions:

1. What's my firm conviction or belief?
2. What do I want the person or people I'm communicating with to know?
3. What do they believe?
4. What do they need to know?
5. What are they ready to hear at this particular time?

Bob would probably have said and done things very differently if he had answered these questions before approaching Mike. Communication isn't only about finding the right words. It's about finding the right way and the right time to say them.

THE PROCESS OF PERSUASION

There's a common myth about storytelling, one where the storyteller believes that getting the audience's attention is the hard part and focuses all his or her energy there. We tend to think that once we have people's' attention, we can deliver the information that will persuade them to decide and then subsequently act. Change doesn't happen like that. People don't always act logically based on what they see and hear. If they did, every child whose family had access to vaccinations would be immunised against life-threatening diseases, smokers would kick their habit and obesity would be in decline. We are not rational actors.

Our mindset can change how we process and perceive information. Professor Robert Cialdini's research in the field of influence and persuasion discovered that people can be primed to be more receptive to a message. Factors like reciprocity, scarcity, authority, consistency, liking, and consensus make us more open to being persuaded. After dinner mints served with the bill can increase how much we tip the waiter. If we perceive something is in limited supply, we want it more. We're more likely to respond positively to professionals who deliberately showcase their expertise, and to people who cooperate with and complement us. It isn't only facts or our conscious minds that are driving or changing our opinions and behaviour; our unconscious mind is also in play.

According to the work of B.J. Fogg, creator of the Fogg Behaviour Model, people need to have the motivation and ability before they can be triggered to change their behaviour. That's why we improve our chances of getting to the gym if we leave our exercise gear out the night before.

It's estimated that between two to three million people die from vaccine preventable diseases every year and that twenty-seven million children don't get the basic course of immunisations, despite the fact that immunisation is a very cost-effective way of improving child survival in developing countries.

✳

Change is a process.
It happens by
degrees, over time.

✳

In India, the immunisation rate is low even though immunisation is free in public health facilities. Researchers at Massachusetts Institute of Technology wanted to find out if they could use small incentives to trigger parents to bring their children to be vaccinated. They carried out their research in the Udaipur district, in rural Rajasthan, India, where less than two percent of one-to two-year-olds received the basic course of immunisations. Five visits to the public health facility are required to complete the full course of immunisations. The team arranged for monthly immunisation camps to be set up in the villages. In addition, one group of parents was offered a kilo of lentils every time they brought their child to be immunised, and a set of thalis (metal serving plates) when the course of immunisations was completed. The lentils were worth less than a dollar, which is the equivalent of three quarters of a day's wages. In villages where reliable immunisation camps were established, completed immunisation rates were 16.6 percent, and in villages where parents were offered lentils, those rates more than doubled to 38.3 percent. Changing how the experience was designed based on what was known about the community's circumstances, mindset and motivations changed the outcome.

THE COMMERCIALISATION OF PERSUASION

On a hot summer afternoon, the tinkling of 'Greensleeves' brought us children running to the corner of Corrib Road, announcing the imminent arrival of the ice cream man. There he would park his van, keeping the engine running, and take orders for soft-serve cones, 99s, screwballs and fruit boats. The ice cream man was one of my first encounters with commercial persuasion in action. The special offer sign Mr Ryan the greengrocer put next to the bread and cream cakes at the end of the day was another. Both are examples of small businesses capturing the attention of existing customers in their neighbourhood or shop. But even as I was growing up, times were changing fast for the ice cream man and Mr Ryan. Increasing competition, accompanied by radio and TV advertising spawned the creation of an entire industry dedicated to mass persuasion. More companies with bigger product ranges all vied to serve the same customers. Vendors believed they had to shout louder to be heard.

But I'm getting ahead of myself. People have been trying to persuade others in commercial settings for thousands of years. Advertising existed long before we had access to a printing press. We know that Egyptians use papyrus to create political posters and Chinese merchants hawked their wares by shouting in the market. During the middle ages in England, a time when many people were illiterate, symbols and graphics were used to advertise services. The invention of the printing press merely accelerated the move to mass persuasion.

It wasn't long before direct mail marketers and radio and TV advertisers realised that a captive audience was not just a means to make a sale, but also a great way to become top of mind. As Ries and Trout famously observe in their book *Positioning*, increasing competition meant that marketers were in a battle for the customer's mind—advertising was used to help a product occupy a 'position' in the mind of the increasingly overwhelmed customer.

*

We don't just persuade people to act. We move them to act.

*

Advertising became an economic powerhouse in capitalist societies of the 19th and 20th centuries, with the advent of direct mail, radio and TV advertising. The commercial persuasion industry blossomed. Marketers who had previously only had the opportunity to persuade face-to-face could now reach more people in more places at scale. Supermarkets could get people's attention by baiting them with special offers with coupons *before* they visited the store. Brands could convince people to try or buy before they encountered their products. Bands could get people excited about their music before they heard it. These new advertising media shifted our perception about how people could be persuaded. For a while advertising was considered the most effective way to influence people.

In many cases, the advertisers' mindset and motivations shifted too. Expectations about what was possible, in what time frame changed. Now that advertising had the potential to reach everyone, companies aimed to capture the attention of the most people. Along with that shift in the mindset and motivations of advertisers, the mechanics of commercial persuasion altered too.

The next big shift happened with the dawn of the digital age, when it became virtually free to reach everyone. The Internet encouraged marketers to go for quick wins. Clicks became currency. Facebook likes had value. Marketing goals changed. Now, instead of investing time to understand customers' unmet needs and unspoken desires as successful companies had been doing for generations, we began to monitor their online behaviour, looking for patterns and vulnerabilities, gathering data to leverage later—sometimes to serve or oftentimes to exploit the user. Virality became top of mind.

Marketers began believing that only the most visible would win. Many of us changed how we spoke to and treated prospective customers, behaving like predators rather than customer advocates. We sacrificed memorability for visibility. We spoke of targeting prospects and winning the war on attention. Our motivations changed along with our language, and naturally our strategies and tactics changed too.

We collected followers. Created clickbait. Counted pageviews. Tracked open rates. The medium not only changed the message, it changed the messenger too. And in the end, the tactics we used made us less effective as communicators and changemakers.

MAKING CHANGE HAPPEN

We have come to believe that our success is dependent on getting the greatest number of people to act on what we're drawing their attention to. The truth is, our ideas succeed when we are trusted and believed by the right people.

James Dyson spent five years perfecting the engineering and design he knew would revolutionise the vacuum cleaner. It had taken persistence on an extraordinary scale, but after creating more than 5,000 prototypes, he was finally ready to share his new technology with the world. He had done the hard part. Once the people who were frustrated with traditional vacuum cleaners saw how much better the Dyson cleaner was, selling it would be a piece of cake.

The first logical step it seemed, would be to approach the companies who were already in the vacuum

✳

*Engagement
is the act of
communicating
with conviction and
empathy to build
trust.*

✳

cleaner business and offer to license the technology to them. They already had established manufacturing facilities, customers, sales teams, marketing capability and distribution channels. He thought all he needed to do was to show them how much better his new cyclone system was than their existing technology, and then negotiate a deal. Dyson approached all of the vacuum companies and domestic appliance manufacturers and secured meetings with most of them. They had 'a good look at it' but were simply not interested in investigating the opportunity further. Dyson's system did away with the need to replace the dust bag that was essential for the conventional vacuum to function. Selling the replaceable dust bags generated considerable revenue for these market leaders. No wonder they were reluctant to change their business model.

When he had exhausted all avenues with manufacturers, Dyson realised that he was wasting his breath. He needed to stop trying to persuade the people who had no interest in disrupting the industry with a better product. He needed to manufacture it himself, selling it directly to the people whose problem he'd been trying to solve all along—the people who wanted cleaner floors.

Dyson eventually convinced the buyer for the biggest mail order catalogue in England to list his product. A second catalogue listing followed, and then department store John Lewis decided to stock Dyson vacuums. The company used product demonstrations to show people why the Dyson vacuum was better, and made them feel smarter for buying one even though it was more expensive. As users began to talk about how good Dyson's were, one by one department stores began to stock them. They were seen as an investment, a product that was built to last. Within two years, the Dyson became the bestselling vacuum cleaner in the UK.

Today Sir James Dyson is known as one of the most successful inventors in British history. He still retains 100 percent ownership of the company, which has gone on to reinvent appliances like fans, hand driers and hairdryers. Dyson posted a $1.1 billion profit in 2017. The brand is known throughout the world for taking an everyday problem and coming up with what many people consider to be a vastly superior solution.

Why weren't the vacuum cleaner manufacturers excited about Dyson's innovative technology? The success of what we make, serve, sell or advocate for is dependent on creating or sustaining change. The same rule applies if we're trying to change perception or behaviour, whether you want to encourage people to try a new product or stop using plastic straws. When we're in selling mode, we prioritise getting **attention** and creating **awareness**. We devote the majority of our resources to making people notice us for a few extra seconds, without always having a plan for how we will convert that attention to action. We spend a lot of our time interrupting our way to awareness—hoping and believing that once people see our solution, they will immediately adopt it. We couldn't be further from the truth. Companies don't thrive on mass awareness. They succeed by moving people from awareness to action and then advocacy.

＊

Communication isn't only about finding the right words. It's about finding the right way and the right time to say them.

＊

PRIMING AND TIMING

We've been exploring the reasons why saying the right thing to the right person improves our chances of getting our ideas across. It's also important to remember how important timing is to effective communication. We've all heard a joke fall flat because it was told to the wrong people at the wrong time. Comedians understand that perfect timing can make or break their act. A punchline only works because the audience is primed for it. The same is true for any message. We become better influencers by understanding our audience's mindset and motivations at a given time.

If you've ever tried to quit a bad habit or establish a new one, you know that change takes time. When it comes to creating change in our own lives, we cut ourselves some slack because we know that change is a process. And yet when it comes to our colleagues and customers, we impatiently hurry them through the process. We try to persuade people to act before they're ready. The result is a failed communication or marketing strategy. The alternative is to understand where your audience or prospective customer is in their change process and to meet them where they are.

For the purpose of this book and our conversation, let's assume that the people you want to build trust with have the motivation and ability to make a decision or change their behaviour, and your goal is to influence or trigger them to decide or change. The following seven stages illustrate how and why people's mindset and motivations can shift as they alter their opinions or behaviour. People are susceptible to being influenced at each of these seven stages of change.

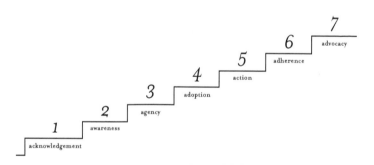

STAGES OF CHANGE

© Bernadette Jiwa

1. **Acknowledgement**

   The person recognises a problem or unmet need.

2. **Awareness**

   The person accepts that change is desirable and possible and begins investigating solutions.

3. **Agency**

   The person becomes confident about their power to create change and more motivated to make a decision.

4. **Adoption**

   The person comes to a decision or becomes committed to a particular solution.

5. **Action**

   The person changes their behaviour or beliefs based on their decision.

6. **Adherence**

   The person sustains the new behaviour, creates habits, or exhibits loyalty.

7. **Advocacy**

   The person develops an affinity for the brand or cause and becomes an ambassador who spreads the word.

✷

Our mindset can change how we process and perceive information.

✷

When we see these stages mapped out, we can understand why vacuum cleaner manufacturers were not immediately persuaded by Dyson's innovative technology. The entire discussion fell apart at the first stage because the manufacturers didn't acknowledge there was a problem. They were not primed to receive the idea. If we're going to open minds and win hearts, we must recognise that communication is never purely an exchange of information with everyone. Our message will fall on deaf ears and closed hearts unless we find a way to make a connection with its intended audience. As author J.K. Rowling said, 'No story lives unless someone wants to listen.' We instigate change by earning the trust of the right listener and empowering them to act. Awareness is necessary, but it's not enough.

THE CHANGE JOURNEY

Victoria Parade, the road that separates Melbourne's northern suburbs from the city is a busy spot. It is used by trams, cars, buses and commuters alike, and dotted at intervals with pedestrian crossings. One of the most popular walking routes across the dual carriageway isn't along the designated path at the traffic lights, it's a shortcut across the grass embankment created by pedestrians where it's most convenient for them to cross.

Shortcuts like these are called *desire paths*. A desire path is usually the most easily navigated route between two places. You've probably seen or even used them in your own town or city. Desire paths often become more useful to local pedestrians than planned footpaths. They tell the story about the journeys taken by the community that made them, and how they decided the way they wanted to go.

Effective sales and marketing are about helping people to do something they already want to do. But just like town planners who design cities to optimise the movement and safety of commuters, changemakers like us must understand that the free will of people will prevail. It's our job to be alongside them on their journey as they decide what's right for them.

In business the customer journey always begins with an awareness that the product exists. Advertising and all other forms of marketing attempt to move people from brand awareness to a sale. Even when we have the knowledge, skills and budget to tell a story that resonates with potential customers, we sometimes end up telling the wrong story. Our mistake lies in trying to get the customer to make the leap from attention to action, from brand awareness to 'buy now', without nurturing them through the steps that help them to feel like they're making an informed decision. We can work in partnership with clients and customers, guiding them through the steps from awareness to advocacy with the help of a tool that I call the Change Journey.

The Change Journey consists of four parts: attention, connection, persuasion, and action. Whatever we serve or sell, our aim is for people to go from knowing about it to investing in, supporting,

＊

*You can
buy attention,
but you can't
buy trust.*

＊

or buying it. We start by making people aware that the idea, product or service exists, but information alone is not usually enough to convince people to buy. They want to reinforce their worldview about the kind of person they are, and the kind of person they dream of being. They need to know they can trust the idea, or the product. They want reassurance that we can be trusted to deliver on the promise. And so, they begin to look for proof that they can. Our role at this stage is to help our audience to do that by building trust and deepening connection with them—not by bombarding them with more information. In our attempt to persuade, we often give people too much information, too soon. It's only once they develop trust in the brand that people are open to investigating whether the product will meet specs and fulfil their needs.

This is the point when they double down on research—looking for more information about pricing, features and benefits that will help them to confirm that they are making the right decision. Prospective customers may compare and contrast products, visit the store to look at the physical product, do a price comparison, or look for other evidence to support their choice. Perhaps they check out product reviews online. Once they are satisfied that they trust the brand and are persuaded that the product is right for them, they will be ready to decide or buy.

Let's think about how this works in practice. When I book a hotel, I search online using my favourite hotel booking platform. If the hotel is listed there, they've got my attention. Once I make a shortlist of hotels, I visit each hotel's website and check TripAdvisor for previous guests' reviews and the management's response to average reviews. This is the point where I'm trying to establish trust in the individual brand. Then I compare prices, hotel locations, facilities and booking flexibility to make sure my specific requirements can be met. I'm narrowing down my choices and am open to being persuaded. Only after I complete my research do I get out my credit card to book the room. If the hotel is not listed with the booking platform, I don't discover it and it doesn't succeed in getting my attention. If the hotel's own website doesn't live up to my expectations and the online guest reviews are poor, then I don't move to the next step of making sure the hotel can meet my requirements. And if the payment process and the user experience upon checkout aren't simple and easy to use, the hotel still risks losing my booking to another provider.

The role of every business is to support the customer to make the right decision. Effective communicators and salespeople do this by understanding what their audience wants and needs to know as they work through their decision. We can use the Change Journey to help us successfully navigate the sales process and meet our customers where they are.

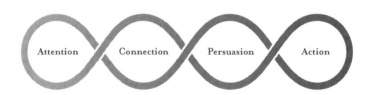

Attention   Connection   Persuasion   Action

THE CHANGE JOURNEY

© Bernadette Jiwa

*

*Our ideas succeed
when we are trusted
and believed by the
right people.*

*

It's important to note that change can happen one person at a time, because the actions of the few are witnessed by the many. This idea was explored by Malcolm Gladwell in his brilliant book, *The Tipping Point*, where he describes how a few of the right people with particular social skills have the power to create social epidemics or make ideas 'tip'.

Gladwell's theory is one way to explain why celebrities and online influencers have become a powerful force in the marketing industry. Of course, the success of any idea or sustainability of any company relies on achieving critical mass, but that success can be achieved without appealing to the masses. In fact, it's increasingly the case that businesses and brands with cult followings begin serving and changing people at the edges. Airbnb enables millions of people to rent a room in the home of hosts they have never met. And yet, millions more would never dream of spending a night in a stranger's bed, preferring instead to stay at a hotel that has a 24-hour receptionist, an in room safe, and an expensive minibar. You might have chosen to read a paperback edition of this book because you love that new book smell, the texture of the pages between your fingers, or the ability to scribble notes in the margin. If you're a Kindle reader, perhaps you like the convenience of being able to take more books with you when you travel, or having your entire library accessible from anywhere. The point is, Amazon didn't need to change the mind of every diehard paperback reader to make the Kindle a success. They needed to present the alternative to enough of the right people, those who were open to trying it and who then told others about how much they loved it.

THE CHANGE GAP

We know it's not possible to inspire people to act or to create change with attention alone. There's always a gap between gaining awareness, enabling action and gaining traction. You can buy attention, but you can't buy trust. Trust is earned. Trust takes time. Trust is the enabler of connection and persuasion. The time between attention and action is what I call the Change Gap. To close this gap, we must first build trust and then reinforce the opinions and beliefs of the audience we're trying to reach. We bridge the gap with connection and persuasion. This is why for example, a hotel's reviews on websites like TripAdvisor can make or break the business. When every hotel has a comfortable bed and free Wi-Fi, prospective guests are looking for another way to differentiate offerings, and reviews enable them to do that.

The act of persuasion gives people the opportunity to confirm whether what they believe is true. Things like providing more and accurate information, product features, measurements, photographs, pricing, demonstrations, reviews or recommendations help people to decide if your product or service is for them.

There are many real world examples of companies who have successfully bridged the Change Gap, and industries that have been spawned by doing so. Think about the products and services we didn't know we wanted but now consume or use regularly. Bottled water, ride-sharing services, reusable coffee cups, coworking spaces, bean-to-bar chocolate, yoga pants, nail bars, coconut oil and meal kits are just a few. The people and companies who convinced so many of us to be open to these products and services bridged the Change Gap by being purposeful storytellers.

THE CHANGE GAP

© Bernadette Jiwa

TWO

Purposeful Storytelling

"Storytelling is the most powerful way to put ideas into the world."
—ROBERT MCKEE

There are only a handful of monuments that most people in the world can imagine in their mind's eye even if they have never visited them. The Eiffel Tower in Paris, the sails of Sydney's Opera House, the Statue of Liberty and San Francisco's Golden Gate Bridge are among them. Of all the thousands of bridges in the world, the Golden Gate is the most memorable. It took four years to build this bridge that

✳

*When we know who
we are, and who
we want to be, to
whom, we tell the
right story.*

✳

spans almost two miles. Eleven men died during its construction. It was painted 'International Orange' to complement its natural surroundings and make it more visible in San Francisco's legendary fog. 112,000 vehicles cross the bridge each day, and more than 10 million people visit it each year. That's an average of more than 27,000 visitors per day—but only around a third of those visitors actually walk across the bridge.

I remember the day when I accidentally became one of them. It was a perfect day during my second visit to San Francisco. A lazy wind accompanied clear skies. The locals told me and my husband how lucky we were with the weather. San Francisco tends to be foggy because of its proximity to the Pacific Ocean and its cold air flow. Fog often covers the top of the majestic Golden Gate Bridge. But the day of our visit wasn't one of those days. We decided to take advantage of the glorious weather and hop on the open-top bus tour of the city. Our driver Dwayne, kept us informed and entertained for the whole trip. He was clearly proud of his city—the only place he had ever called home. As we were nearing the end of our tour, before we headed back over the bridge, he pulled into a parking spot and stopped the bus so he could 'address his guests'. Like an actor about to deliver the most important performance of his life, Dwayne stood tall, facing the audience seated in the rows of the bus behind him, and invited us to turn around and look around at the iconic bridge.

He started by telling us why he loved the city he had called home for almost 60 years. He regarded his job sharing the city with visitors, as both a pleasure and a privilege. And then he began evangelising the stunning monument we were about to drive across.

'This bridge will be the standard for every bridge that will ever be built,' he said. 'They say Disneyland is magical. No, this bridge is magical! Even guys take selfies on this bridge.'

Dwayne acknowledged that it was a cold day, but reminded us that we were in San Francisco at a beautiful time to experience the sights. We might not get a single clear day the next time we visited. He told us that although he drives across the bridge every day, he walks across it on the weekend whenever he can.

And then he invited us to get off the bus and do the same. Not because we had to—Dwayne was about to drive the bus across anyway—but because we could.

'Maybe you think it's too cold. Maybe you're telling yourself that you'll do it next time. But there may not be a next time. And one day when you get home, and you're showing the photos of your trip to friends, they will ask you if you walked across the bridge. Your trip will be defined by your answer to that question.'

Then Dwayne stood back and gave us a moment to decide. Half of the passengers, many of whom would have left a tip in the tip jar on the dashboard when their trip ended at the next stop, left the bus to walk across the magnificent Golden Gate Bridge, as our guide got back in his seat, turned the ignition and drove away.

Most of us fail to engage with people the way Dwayne did with us, a bus full of near strangers that day. We fall into unhelpful communication habits because we're looking for a shortcut to the outcome we want. Like any habit these behaviour patterns

✳

*How we connect
and persuade is
affected by the way
we choose to deliver
the message.*

✳

are crutches we lean on—a default way of thinking and acting we repeat that might not serve us in the long run.

In situations where we're trying to persuade, one of the habits we fall into is only seeing the world through our lens. Whether we're encouraging our kids to get dressed for school or convincing our customers to choose a product, we tend to begin with our own ends in mind. Our communication strategy then mainly focusses on what we want the person on the receiving end of our message to do. So we work backwards from there, looking for the quick route to a resolution, reaction or sale. Our impatience leads us to tell the wrong story—we end up using tactics that feel inauthentic or desperate and that inevitably lose the people we hope to engage.

Think back to how Dwayne persuaded us to get off the warm bus and walk across the Golden Gate Bridge on a cold day. He built trust with us over the time we were on the tour. He connected with us every step of the way, telling us stories about the area that we wouldn't have heard anywhere else, and giving us tips about where to eat and shop. He put in the work of standing in our shoes and imagining what we would think, feel, say and do when we got home. Then he narrated our story back to us. He painted a picture of what it would feel like to have walked across the bridge. He did that by considering our mindset and motivations. Then Dwayne used his storytelling skills as the trigger to encourage us to do the thing he knew we'd be glad we did.

The opportunity to be as good a storyteller as Dwayne is open to all of us. Powerful, purposeful storytellers like Dwayne have three things in common:

1. They have a conviction about the change they're trying to create.
2. They know who they want to take with them on that journey.
3. They tell a story that supports them in achieving that goal.

Whenever you're moved by an advertisement or find yourself choosing to pay more for something because of how its designed, look for the purposeful story that caused your response.

- What was the brand's conviction?
- How did they appeal to and reinforce your worldview?
- Whose worldview did they ignore?
- How did they tell a story that supported them in achieving their goal?

When we know who we are, and who we want to be, to whom, we tell the right story.

START HERE

On our thirtieth wedding anniversary, my husband gave me a gift—he had collected the cards and letters from the first flush of our love affair. The Valentine's card he sent me in 1986 was still tucked inside the envelope with the date stamp on it. He kept the handwritten love letters we sent every day that summer when he was a medical student, doing an elective in London as part of his training. We laughed as we read our younger selves arranging call times days in advance, and recounting the need to have enough five and ten pence coins to feed the phone boxes in the corridors of our respective apartment

✳

*We can be fearfully
reactive to the
marketplace or
bravely responsive
to our customers.*

✳

buildings. Back then we never could have imagined the giant technological leap that would be made in just a couple of decades. We didn't foresee how it would change the way we all stay connected, or in some cases have become disconnected.

Throughout history, the technology of the day has always influenced how its users communicate and share ideas. How we think about spreading ideas is shaped by the resources available to us. How we connect and persuade is affected by the way we choose to deliver the message. When we're face-to-face, we gesture and embellish. When we're tweeting or texting, we use emoji and cut to the chase.

Our behaviour isn't the only thing that changed over time. A subtle change in our mindset simultaneously took place too. We began to focus less on the drivers of change—the reasons behind those interactions we initiated. And we started to prioritise the immediate benefit we wanted to get from the interaction. We neglected to build trust before sharing the message and instead obsessed over just delivering it. The result is that we have changed from purposeful storytellers, who care about how the audience or user feels, to pragmatic communicators who prioritise 'getting the word out there' so we can persuade people to act.

The problem with just homing in on the mode of delivery is that technology is constantly changing. No sooner have you conquered the Facebook marketing landscape than the algorithm changes. One minute it seems that print is dead; then suddenly the tangible is having a revival. The answer then, is not to get too preoccupied with adapting your message to suit the changing technology of the day, but to focus on what's *unchanging* about *people* instead.

So, where should your story begin? There's a tendency to dedicate the bulk of our resources—time, energy and money—to the delivery of our messages. But effective storytelling happens in two parts. Purposeful storytelling is a combination strategy and tactics. You must define your strategy before you begin designing and deploying tactics. You have to know *who* you want to influence and *why*—to be clear about what's driving your story, before you consider *what, where, when* and *how* you're going to deliver the message to those people you hope to reach and change. Starting with the why is important because if we focus only on the how, the delivery, then our stories fall flat and we are less likely to create the change we hope to make.

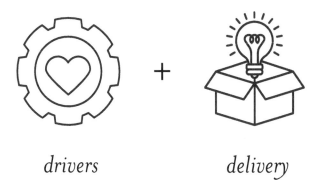

drivers   *delivery*

✳

*Purposeful
storytellers
and effective
changemakers have
a strong conviction
about the change
they're trying to
create.*

✳

THE STORY COMPASS

One in ten people worldwide don't have access to clean drinking water. That's 663 million people worldwide who are at risk of dying from diseases caused by dirty water. Of the deaths that are caused by these diseases, 43 percent are children under five. Access to clean water can save around 16,000 lives every week. In Africa alone, women spend 40 billion hours a year walking for water. Every $1 invested in clean water can yield $4–$12 in economic returns.

The facts are hard to dispute, the potential impact of a donation is obvious, and yet donors are sceptical. Armed with data like this, you'd think it would be easy for charities to persuade people to donate to good causes. But marketing tactics that rely on interrupting people–without first earning their permission and trust—are still routinely used by non-profits today. The charity fundraisers I met as I walked home from the city are usually stationed in pairs at the street corners outside the university. They stand there from 9am until 3pm hoping to stop and then convince passers-by (mainly university students like them) to sign up and become regular donors. Most people rush past them head down, earbuds in, avoiding eye contact. Others smile weakly, gesturing to imaginary watches on their wrists, indicating that they're in a hurry. Many seem irritated by the interruption.

The fundraisers average five to seven signups on a good day. That's one donor per hour gained for the charity. For some, this might seem like an effective marketing strategy, but there are other factors to consider here. What's the donor retention rate? How many people who feel pressured into saying yes on the pavement end up cancelling? Could the charity get a better result by deploying those marketing resources more creatively, to build affinity instead of competing for attention? How much damage does interrupting people do to their brand? Are they telling the right story?

We've come to a crossroads in sales and marketing. We have two choices. We can be fearfully reactive to the marketplace or bravely responsive to our customers. We can carry on doing what we've been doing since the golden days of advertising and the

Madison Avenue era. We can spend more money interrupting more people in physical and digital places—with the intention of finding the quickest route from getting everyone's attention to making a tiny percentage of people act. Or we can find a group of people we want to serve, people with a need or a desire we care about fulfilling, and earn their trust and loyalty over time. We must choose whether we want to make weak ties by going broad and shallow, or strong ties by going narrow and deep. We need to decide if we want to be the loudest or most resonant, most visible or most memorable. We can't be both.

Every day, probably many times a day, you're trying to engage with people. A conversation at the bus stop, a quick email, the delivery note sent inside the package, your last Instagram post and the way you greet a customer, are all acts of engagement. Your goal is to help people to understand, remember and often act on your message. On a good day, it's easier to be a purposeful storyteller. On a day when you're overstretched, it's harder to consistently align your intention and message.

✴

Our culture is changed not only because of what we do but by the way we do it. How we do things becomes our legacy.

✴

That's why I created the Story Compass—to help you and your team navigate your storytelling terrain.

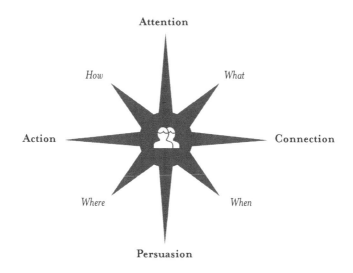

THE STORY COMPASS

© Bernadette Jiwa

The Story Compass is a simple communication tool designed to facilitate powerful, purposeful storytelling. In essence, the Story Compass clarifies your understanding about where you want your story to take your audience, and guides the actions that will bring them with you on the journey. It enables you to define your story strategy and design your tactics.

While it's one tool, as I explain how to use it here, I'll break it down into two parts. First, we'll look at Story Drivers, and then we'll look at Story Delivery.

Story Drivers: Define Your Strategy

Story Drivers shape your communication strategy. They are the **why** of your story. The direction you want the message to take you and your audience. It's helpful to think of Story Drivers as the route to your destination. When we're in a hurry to create change, it's tempting to focus impatiently on our end goal. We sometimes act as if the mere fact of knowing where we want to go will get us there. The truth is that we can't change things without knowing what the person we're hoping to change already believes and believes in. So your story's first key driver must be **who**. You must consider the beliefs and aspirations of your intended audience before you begin to communicate what you want them to know.

The reason our stories, messaging and marketing fall flat is that the people we want to serve are not motivated by our need to be seen, to be heard or to close a sale. People—your audience, customers and clients—are motivated by their need to be seen, heard and understood. We all are.

These are some of the questions you need to answer about who you are hoping to change:

- Who do you want to influence?
- What's the change you're helping them to undergo?
- What do they believe?
- What do they want to do, but think they can't?
- What's the unmet need you're helping them to fulfil?
- What are their unspoken desires?
- Who will they become in the presence of your product?
- How can you align your goals with their aspirations?
- Why should they trust you?

These were the sorts of questions Scott Harrison CEO of charity: water and his team addressed before they began to create a storytelling strategy that

✳

A message that resonates relies on the communicator discerning the most effective way to deliver it.

✳

would resonate with potential donors. Harrison was convinced that there had to be a better fundraising model for non-profits, and he set out to create it. He believed that radical transparency was the key to earning donors' trust.

The data about attitudes to giving backed up Scott's belief. People don't trust charities. Only one in ten Americans believes that charities are honest and ethical. People wonder how much of their contribution reaches the people in need. They are concerned about the proportion of it that's used to pay for administrative work or the fundraising efforts themselves. If charity: water was to achieve their goal of bringing clean water to everyone, they needed to tell a better story. It wasn't enough to tell people what they were doing with donations. They had to bridge the Change Gap by showing them too.

Scott and his team did this by partnering with philanthropists who agreed to finance the administration of the charity, allowing 100 percent of all public donations to fund water projects. The next step in their model was to show where every dollar went, using photos and GPS coordinates. They invested in experienced local organisations to help them build the right infrastructure to fund sustainable community owned water projects around the world.

At present, charity: water has more than 28,000 water projects up and running, bringing clean water to 8 million people in 26 countries. While trust in charities has been falling, charity: water has managed to build trust by showing people exactly where their donations go, thus helping them to have faith in supporting the cause. As the charity: water team began to understand their potential donors' mindset, motivations and objections they knew that they would need to build proof and accountability into their donations model. Once people were reassured that their money was being directed to where it was needed most, they were comfortable about donating and fundraising for charity: water.

When you understand your audience's **mindset**—what they think, feel, say and do—and their **motivation**—what they *would like to* think, feel, say and do—then you can begin to tell stories that resonate with them.

As we set out to influence our target audience, we sometimes overlook the role and the needs of the other equally important **who** of our story—the *second* 'who' is **you**. Purposeful storytellers and effective changemakers have a strong conviction about the change they're trying to create. You need to know where you're headed before you plot your course and set sail. Being clear about your conviction enables you to speak in a way that will attract the right people and perhaps more importantly, allow you to ignore the people you can't and won't influence or change.

The clarity with which you show up, as only you can, changes how the story is told and with whom it resonates. How you go about your work can have just as much impact on your results as the work itself. Our culture is changed not only because of *what* we do but by *the way* we do it. How we do things becomes our legacy. It might sound blindingly obvious to say that you should believe and be invested in the change you're trying to create. But it's not unheard of for someone to reach a goal—to scale a corporate ladder, launch a company or invest resources in serving a

＊

Storytelling is as much about showing as it is about telling.

＊

particular client—only to realise that the path they've been on isn't the right path for them. And while I could write a whole other book about doing the right work for the right reasons, I'd simply like to call it out here in the context of how we create change. It's likely that we have a better chance of creating positive change for others when our work fulfils us too. You can choose to save your best work for the projects and people where you can make the most difference.

As you look at the Story Compass, you will see that the audience—the who, your number one driver is at its centre. The four other key Story Drivers correspond with the four parts of the Change Journey: attention, connection, persuasion and action. You can't change a mind or win a heart unless someone is ready, willing and able to be persuaded or to act. You must meet the audience where they are.

Attention: If people are not interested in your message, they won't connect with your cause or brand.

Connection: If people don't trust you, they won't be persuaded by you.

Persuasion: If people don't understand the benefit to them, they won't be persuaded to act.

Action: When people know, trust and understand why they should act, they do.

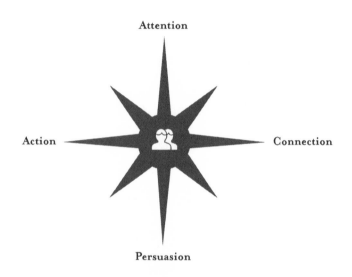

STORY DRIVERS

© Bernadette Jiwa

Before you begin to craft your message, you need to decide if the purpose of that message is to get **attention** or to deepen trust and **connection**. Is it to empower people to be open to **persuasion** or to act?

Perhaps it's some combination of all four drivers. Story Drivers serve as your reminder about the job you're asking the story to do. Your story strategy will be more effective because you've reflected on the why of your story and what success looks like. In the case of charity: water for example, we saw how building trust with potential donors influenced not only the non-profit's communications strategy, but its entire brand strategy. This in turn impacted donors' attitudes not only to giving, but to confidently spreading the word about the charity they trusted.

Story Delivery: Design and Deploy Your Tactics

Once you know why you're telling the story you can begin to work on how to best tell it. The tactics you use to get your message across are the **how** of your story—the means by which you carry out your strategy. What you say and do, when and where, has an impact on where you end up. A message that resonates relies on the communicator discerning the most effective way to deliver it.

*

*Powerful,
purposeful stories
are a combination
of strategy and
tactics.*

*

Our neighbours recently had the outside of their house painted. It's a Victorian property, built in the 1800s with period features and delicate ironwork. I watched the decorators come and go during the weeks they were completing the job. They took care to cover the original tiles on the porch which could so easily be damaged. They arrived on time and worked diligently. Several of the neighbours who passed by admired their work and asked for a business card.

I'm sure the decorators have a website, and I'm also pretty confident that they convert more enquiries from the top of their ladders than they do from the contact form on their site. Sometimes the opportunity to tell the right story to the right people is hidden in plain sight.

It's tempting to think about storytelling as a way of delivering information using words on a page, either physical or digital. But storytelling is as much about showing as it is about telling. We have the opportunity to engage people's five senses and we should use it. Before we deliver an effective message, we must consider which tactics are appropriate in which situation.

- How can we best engage with our audience?
- What's the best medium to use?
- When is the best time to deliver the message?
- Where is the best place to deliver the message?

STORY DELIVERY

© Bernadette Jiwa

The HOW of Your Story

The communication tactics you use in a specific situation can help you to drive change. These include things like print advertising, product giveaways, group meetings, a private conversation, a pitch, phone call, email, video, a tweet, word of mouth, a recommendation or a review. Loyalty programs, content creation, blogs, podcasts, hosting and sponsoring events, webinars, online groups and open source software platforms. Bear in mind that sometimes you aren't the person controlling the message. Your customers or audience are sharing the story through reviews and recommendations—which is why it's important to give them a story to tell.

The WHAT of Your Story

The tools and the media that will support you in communicating your message might be words, images, data collection, design or price. This is where you get more specific about the best communication tactics to use to convey your message. What should you say? What's the best way to say it?

*The most successful
brand stories are
not for everyone.*

The WHEN of Your Story

When is the best time to deliver the message for it to have maximum impact? We often overlook the importance of timing in communication. We need to avoid starting too early or being too late, communicating too often or not often enough. People are more receptive to being influenced at some times than others. It's vital to understand how the timing of your message could affect your audience's response to it. Timing can either be carefully planned or spontaneous.

In the field of education, unplanned opportunities to convey insight to a student in the classroom are known as 'teachable moments.' People are often more open to particular messages in times of transition or change, like marriage, career shifts and birthdays. Examples of planned timing include linking health screening campaigns to milestones like significant birthdays, marketing diet foods and gym memberships in January, and seasonal merchandising.

Unplanned or opportunistic timing of messages includes 'newsjacking', taking advantage of current events to promote or advertise your product or brand. Yet sometimes jumping on a real-time marketing bandwagon is counterproductive because your message gets lost in the noise.

Should you communicate your message at the start of the month or the end of the week? When is your audience paying attention in general, not just to your message? How are you measuring your audience's responsiveness to the timing of your messages? In a data rich world, there has never been a better time to understand when your audience is paying attention.

The WHERE of Your Story

Not only location but circumstances may give you the best chance of conveying your message and achieving your goals. Geography and tradition can influence where you choose to show up to tell your story. It's no accident that the designer stores in New York are located on Fifth Avenue in Manhattan. To begin with, know where your audience spends time. Are they online or offline? What places do they avoid? Could you design a place where your best customers would want to gather? Have you earned their permission or are you simply spamming them?

Power and status roles also play a part in how your message is perceived and received. Your place in the corporate hierarchy can affect how you communicate with people and how receptive they are to your message. Celebrity endorsement is a popular way for brands to leverage the status and popularity of a trusted influencer's platform to get the word out about their products and services. The voice that delivers the story has the ability to make the idea both travel and stick. When a duchess chooses to carry a particular designer handbag on an official royal engagement that brand immediately garners media attention and increased sales.

Powerful, purposeful stories are a combination of strategy and tactics. Using the Story Compass will help you to ask better questions about what kind of change you're trying to create and plan the best way to go about achieving it.

✳

*How we lead,
changes how people
respond and what
happens next.*

✳

CONVICTION AND COURAGE

The most successful brand stories are not for everyone. If you want to appeal to the right people you have to be willing to repel the wrong people. Brands that successfully bridge the Change Gap resonate deeply with those people they want to influence and serve.

Unless you're an American football fan, you probably hadn't heard of Colin Kaepernick before August 2016. Kaepernick an African American, was a quarterback for the San Francisco 49ers when he was propelled into the media spotlight for choosing to sit and later to kneel during the United States national anthem at the start of NFL games. Kaepernick was protesting racial injustice and alleged police brutality towards African Americans. His controversial actions divided the nation. In a deeply proud and patriotic nation, Kaepernick's protest was seen by some including the country's president, as an insult to the flag and the armed forces. To many he became a hero. Despite the controversy surrounding Kaepernick 'taking a knee' during the anthem, other players followed his lead. Their pregame protests began to dominate the news during 2017, when the country's president publicly criticised the players' actions. Ultimately Kaepernick, who was thrust into the international spotlight as a result paid a heavy price for his activism, opting out of his 49ers contract early because he believed they did not intend to renew it. At the time of writing he has yet to be signed by another team.

On 3rd September 2018, Nike revealed their new advertising campaign featuring Kaepernick. The words, 'Believe in something. Even if it means sacrificing everything,' appeared on billboards across America, followed by Nike's 'Just do it' slogan. The reaction in the media was instant. People who deeply opposed Kaepernick's stance and his activism took to social media to criticise the company. The U.S. president questioned what Nike was thinking in a tweet. Experts debated the wisdom or recklessness of Nike's decision to make Kaepernick the face of their campaign. Analysts watched the company's share price and sales—looking for confirmation that its new, seemingly risky marketing message had harmed their brand.

Nike's mission is 'to bring inspiration and innovation to every athlete in the world.' The company's conviction is that they can change how people feel about what it's possible for them to achieve when they wear the Nike logo. Nike's decision about what story to tell was based on their beliefs about who they are as a company, and what change they seek to create for whom. They followed through on that, knowing that their decision to make Kaepernick a prominent Nike ambassador would polarise people. In choosing to come out in support of a social movement, Nike made a values-based business decision. Many saw it as a gamble, a marketing strategy that could hurt the brand.

Marketing analyst Professor Scott Galloway declared Nike's decision as 'genius'—the 'most gangster marketing move of 2018.' According to Galloway, the Kaepernick campaign also stacks up commercially. He estimates that of Nike's $35 billion in annual revenue, $20 billion is generated overseas. Two thirds of Nike consumers are under 35 years old. They are likely to live in urban areas and have above average disposable income and a progressive worldview. Extrapolating from this data, Galloway says that Nike risked \$1-\$3 billion in revenue to deepen their connection with customers who represent \$32-\$34 billion in revenue. Powerful, strategic stories not only resonate, they are good for business too.

THREE

Purposeful Stories

"We have to go where people are if we're going to get them to somewhere better."

—SETH GODIN

GOING NARROW AND DEEP

Afew years back, I had an email from my friend Mark Dyck, who then owned a neighbourhood bakery with his wife Cindy in Regina, Saskatchewan. He'd been offered the opportunity to advertise his business in *Fine Lifestyles Regina*, a glossy magazine that was delivered to affluent neighbourhoods and upmarket hotels in the city. The ad would cost him $3,000.

Mark is not only a baker, he's a community builder. He has lived in the same place for thirty years. He's a giver and contributor, a friend and a doer. Mark is the kind of guy who doesn't mind taking the long way around. He rolls up his sleeves and gets stuck in. So, something about the idea of passively placing this kind of advert, to get attention from people who were likely not his ideal customers, didn't seem to align with his usual way of doing things. If I were to describe the plan in 'marketing speak', I'd say it felt 'off-brand.' The question I asked Mark in response to his email was this: What could you do for your customers with that $3,000? Mark decided not to place the ad. What he did instead was one of the most thoughtful bits of marketing I've come across. He stocked a basket with a week's supply of delicious fresh bread and gave it away to a loyal customer. But Mark didn't stop there. Instead of choosing a customer at random to receive the basket each week, Mark invited the family who had received it the week before to nominate the next person to get the basket. He kept a 'true friends' photo gallery in the bakery with pictures of the lucky families who were nominated for the basket, along with a notebook where the givers wrote about why they had chosen their friends, neighbours or co-workers to receive the basket. People weren't used to receiving gifts outside of Christmas or birthdays, especially not from their friends. The act of receiving a gift for 'no reason' other than friendship was unexpected and sometimes overwhelming. Many of these people had been friends for a long time but rarely expressed their gratitude out loud. One thing that struck Mark was the anticipation that receivers had about passing the basket along. They were moved by receiving the basket but were even more excited about the opportunity to give it. Who they would pick, what they would say?

The last edition of *Fine Lifestyles Regina* was published in 2015. I doubt if the people of Regina really miss it. But I do know that when Mark and Cindy sold their bakery they were missed. And the story and the impact of the 'true friends bread basket' lives on.

As leaders of families, communities and companies, and as marketers of products, services and ideas—

we tend to focus our storytelling efforts on getting attention and creating calls to action. We've had decades of practice at mass marketing. We've gotten pretty good at knowing what will get us a moment of awareness. But as I pointed out earlier, no business thrives on attention alone. What Mark did with 'true friends' and the bread basket is what I'm inviting you to use the Story Compass to do. To take the harder, and perhaps longer route—the one most people aren't prepared to take. To be assertive, authentic and generous as you navigate your way to making the change you want to make. To prioritise the needs of only those people you want to take with you on that journey. To stop trying to market to everyone.

How we lead, changes how people respond and what happens next. Culture is altered when someone shows up with conviction, bringing their unique abilities, pointing to a way forward and inviting people to embark on that journey with them. We have the power to create the interactions, organisations and places that shape the future we want to see.

Now let's look at some examples of how people, companies and communities who successfully bridged the Change Gap in a variety of different situations and settings. You'll notice as you read through the examples how each of the Story Drivers and Story Delivery points on the Story Compass come into play in each instance. The following stories mainly highlight two Story Drivers, connection and persuasion, because they are the key drivers to bridge the Change Gap.

HOW QANTAS CALMED 300 PASSENGERS IN FIVE MINUTES

A flight from New York to LA with connections to several destinations in Australia was delayed. Cabin crew needed to convey the information about logistics prior to the flight landing in LA.

Drivers

To make sure passengers had the information they needed to make it to their connecting flight and allay their anxiety about the delay, so that they would feel reassured and remain calm towards the end of their journey. The cabin crew had been serving and communicating with the passengers for the entire flight. Their main Story Driver, as they dealt with communicating the logistics of the delay, was **persuasion**. They needed to persuade people to remain calm.

Delivery

Passengers aboard the delayed flight were anxious about catching their connecting flights to their final destinations in Australia. I've been in this situation a number of times. While flight delays are a routine part of travelling, they still make people nervous. All of the 'what if' scenarios start playing out in the travellers' minds. The tension on the aircraft is always palpable. Usually, one or two passengers corner the cabin crew asking for information that's then passed through the cabin in whispers. Most passengers are not reassured because the story is coming to them second hand. This has the added effect of making people a bit panicky and restless. When the aircraft lands, the disembarkation can feel a bit like every man for himself. In an attempt to get to their connecting flights in an airport they probably don't know, passengers abandon travel etiquette. They don't allow the people in the rows in front of them to exit if they hesitate for a moment or are collecting bags. There's pushing and shoving. The atmosphere becomes fraught and chaotic.

This time was different because the cabin crew prioritised the timing of the message's delivery. They realised that **when** and **how** they made the announcement could change things for the better. The customer service manager on our flight made an announcement an hour before we landed. He called out the connecting flight numbers, destinations and gates. He told us how far away the gates were and in which directions. He explained that the ground crew knew we were late and they were holding our flights. His announcement came from a place of empathy. His ability to stand in the passengers' shoes changed how he was driven to tell the story. His tactic was to deliver the same message to everyone once—rather than over and over again to the individuals who happened to ask—and to give us more information than we needed, which was exactly what the audience wanted in this situation.

Outcome

The mood on the aircraft changed in an instant. Passengers were reassured, happier and more relaxed. Disembarkation was a breeze.

HOW ICELAND CHANGED TEEN CULTURE

In 1998 rates of teenage alcohol consumption in Iceland were extremely high. Of the 15- to 16-year-olds surveyed, 42 percent reported being drunk the previous month, 23 percent were smoking cigarettes and 17 percent using cannabis.

Drivers

The Icelandic government wanted to reduce substance abuse and antisocial behaviour amongst teenagers, thus improving the health and wellbeing of the teens and future generations. The journey to Iceland's prevention strategy was backed by the work and research of psychologists Gudberg Jónsson and Harvey Milkman.

In 1992 teenagers in every school in Iceland between the age of fourteen and sixteen were surveyed (the surveys were repeated in 1995 and

1997). They were asked if they had tried alcohol, smoked cigarettes or used cannabis in the previous month. The researchers questioned them about their extracurricular activities and asked if they had a close relationship with their parents. The data revealed patterns that showed the kind of teens who were at risk of substance abuse. Factors that protected against these behaviours were also revealed—not being outdoors late at night, regular participation in organised sports, time spent with parents and feeling nurtured and valued at school.

When the first surveys were undertaken, government substance abuse prevention initiatives focussed mainly on education, warning teenagers about the dangers of drinking and drug abuse. These education programs were not working. Simply having a messaging strategy that communicated the risk of substance abuse was not enough to change behaviour. Awareness of the information wasn't enough to empower teens to make better choices. So, the government, researchers and community needed to prioritise **connection** as they tried to bridge the Change Gap.

Delivery

Armed with this data, the government introduced the Youth in Iceland initiative. State funding for organised extracurricular activities was increased. The law was changed, making it illegal to buy alcohol if you were under twenty and illegal to buy tobacco if you were under eighteen. Advertising of tobacco and alcohol was banned. A law was passed banning 13- to 16-year-olds from being out after 10pm in winter and after midnight in summer. The government strengthened links between parents and schools. Education programs that helped parents to understand the importance of spending quality time with their teenagers were introduced. Parents were encouraged to get to know more about what was going on in their children's lives and who their friends were. Parents could also voluntarily sign agreements committing to creating specific boundaries around drugs and alcohol for their teenagers.

It's clear that the substance abuse problem among Iceland's teens was complex and had to be tackled using a multi-faceted approach. A variety of **how, what, when and where** tactics were used to reinforce the message.

Outcome

By 2016 alcohol consumption in 15- to 16-year-olds fell from 42 to 5 percent. Cigarette smoking among the group was down from 23 to 3 percent and cannabis use fell from 17 to 7 percent. Between 1997 and 2012, the percentage of teenagers aged 15 and 16 who participated regularly in organised sports increased from 24 to 42 percent. The number who reported spending time with their parents on weekdays doubled.

HOW MECCA BUILT A SUCCESSFUL GLOBAL BRAND ONE CUSTOMER AT A TIME

There are thousands of new and innovative beauty brands and products introduced to the market every year. It's hard for women to keep track of them, and even harder to know which ones are better and work best for them.

Drivers

Entrepreneur Jo Horgan wanted to build a cosmetic brand that enabled customers to look and feel their best, 'The idea was to bring these innovative brands into a service-driven, luxury boutique environment where women could shop across all brands and customise the product offer to suit their specific needs and wants.' Her plan was twofold. She wanted to gain a deep understanding of the customers' needs and garner a loyal following by curating the best beauty products on the planet and bringing them to those customers.

Horgan's goal was 'to take someone from a beauty novice to feeling like an expert in a single session, and for a makeup artist to feel like they had found their nirvana—we really wanted everyone to feel welcome, in control and walking out having had a great time.' Being trusted by her customers was key. **Connection** and persuasion were the key drivers of Mecca's strategy.

Delivery

When Horgan launched Mecca Cosmetica in Australia in 1997, she sought out and curated the best (sometimes undiscovered) beauty products on the planet. The **how** would involve offering a high-touch service that over time became uncharacteristic of the digital age. Today Mecca customers can buy a $100 makeup lesson that includes products to the value of $100. The customer spends an hour in the chair with a qualified technician who listens to her beauty needs and problems, providing solutions and product recommendations. The customer also gets to see what the products look and feel like on her skin and learns how to use them. The makeup artist shows women how to make the best of themselves and has a whole hour to connect with customers, gathering information that helps Mecca to personalise their marketing and tailor their services to the customer's needs. This enables the recommendations to be made based on what the customer says, and not on what the company thinks she wants. The timing of the sales conversation the **when**, is crucial to Mecca's success.

Outcome

Mecca started out with a single store in the suburbs of Melbourne. Today the company has grown to eighty stores and counting in Australia and New Zealand with 2,300 employees.

HOW AIRBNB ENABLED TRUST AND CHANGED THE HOSPITALITY INDUSTRY

Airbnb, the online home sharing and hospitality marketplace, launched in 2008 in San Francisco. When a year later the service wasn't doing as well in New York as the founders had hoped, two of the co-founders, Joe Gebbia and Brian Chesky, headed to New York. They stayed in Airbnb listings to see if they could determine the source of the problem. When Gebbia and Chesky arrived, they found that hosts were doing a great job of presenting their listings. The problem was that the photos accompanying the listings on the website didn't reflect how great they were. Hosts weren't attracting guests because they weren't telling their stories as well as they could.

Drivers

The Airbnb founders were thinking about how much and what kind of information a traveller would need in order to trust a stranger enough to book a room in their home. It's likely that prospective guests have a couple of unanswered questions in the back of their minds before they book. How do I know I can trust this person? Will this place be a dive? Airbnb's founders needed to increase hosts' bookings by helping guests to get answers to these questions. They knew they had to help their hosts to earn the trust of prospective guests, so **connection** was their key driver.

It was only after they stayed in 24 of the listings in New York that the founders realised the problem wasn't with the listings, but with how they were being marketed.

Delivery

Instead of sending an email to hosts, telling them to take better photos Gebbia and Chesky rented an expensive camera, using it to take photos of as many New York listings as they could. In 2010, Airbnb partnered with professional photographers and offered hosts the opportunity to schedule an appointment to have their listings photographed. (Airbnb funded this service until 2017; it is now charged to hosts.)

Outcome

Bookings doubled, and in some cases tripled on the listings that had been 'professionally' photographed. This resulted in a doubling of revenue from New York listings the month after the founders' visited the hosts. A professionally photographed listing is two and a half times more likely to be booked. The company went from having just 20 partner photographers in 2010 to 2000 in 2012.

HOW LULULEMON CREATED THE ACTIVEWEAR REVOLUTION

It's hard to remember back to a time not so long ago, when we exercised or went to the gym in our worst clothes. It made sense to wear that ancient, faded t-shirt and those baggy jogging pants—we were just getting sweaty after all. Chip Wilson, the founder of Lululemon forever changed how millions of people felt about what they wore and how they looked while exercising when he launched the yoga inspired athletic apparel brand in 1999.

Drivers

Chip Wilson grew up playing a lot of sports in his native Canada. His father was a physical education teacher and his mother was a seamstress. When he graduated college in the late 1970s, he built a small business designing and making long, colourful, baggy shorts for men. It just so happened that skateboarders loved the shorts that covered their knees. Wilson's brand, Westbeach began making and selling apparel for the global surfing, skateboarding and snowboarding markets. He sold that company in the 1990s.

Wilson's background designing performance sportswear stood him in good stead when he accidentally discovered yoga in 1997. Within a month he realised that yoga was becoming popular really fast. Wilson knew he could design yoga wear that performed well and looked better than the old, worn out gear women were wearing to practice. His lightbulb moment was understanding that if he could produce yoga clothing that was functional *and* made women look and feel good before, during and after practice, he'd be onto something. Wilson came at the problem from the technical angle and added fashion sense. A big part of his product development, sales and marketing strategy was to understand how women wanted to feel and design a product that connected them to that feeling. **Connection** first, **persuasion** second.

Delivery

As he was designing and iterating, Wilson used his yoga instructor as a sounding board. His focus was to make a superior product that was functional and fashionable. From the start Lululemon met customers where they were. Wilson held design meetings with groups of women to perfect fit and importantly see how women reacted to the garments when they touched and wore them.

The first Lululemon store Wilson opened was in downtown Vancouver. The only snag was that it was on the second floor; customers would need a reason to visit because there was nothing to see from the street. So he and his yoga instructor ran their businesses in tandem. Wilson's store became a yoga studio in the morning and evening. The yoga apparel was displayed on rolling racks at the side of the studio during classes. Wilson deliberately chose not to advertise. He intentionally set out to build the Lululemon brand by word of mouth. Lululemon still runs free yoga classes in many of its stores. Wilson believed that his brand would experience a tipping point, but he knew it would have to come from the early adopters of his product. Once women touched and tried the yoga pants on they didn't need to be persuaded to buy them. Lululemon's sales and marketing tactics (the **how, what, when** and **where**) focused on getting the product into the hands of a small and motivated target market.

Lululemon went public in 2007. Wilson stepped down as company chairman in 2013. The company still maintains strong partnerships with the local yoga communities where their stores are, and they have an ambassador program, giving products to their network of sponsored yoga instructors.

Outcome

By April 2018, Lululemon had over 400 stores and employed more than 13,000 people. The global sports and fitness clothing market is expected to reach over $230 billion by 2024. Lululemon's revenue is projected to be $4 billion by 2020. It's estimated that more than 36 million people in the U.S. practice yoga.

HOW HOTELS GET US TO REUSE TOWELS

Every day in hotels across the world guests are using a freshly laundered, fluffy towel only once. Then they drop it on the floor never to use it again, despite the fact that they will be staying in the same room that night. It's estimated that laundry takes up 16 percent of a hotel's water usage. Hotels want to encourage people to reuse their towels to save water, cut labour costs, and reduce their environmental impact. Most hotels have a towel reuse program in place, but guest participation varies. In 2012 a report estimated that towel reuse in UK hotels was as low as 5 percent.

Drivers

Hotels want to **persuade** guests to reuse towels. Hoteliers need to find a relatively quick route from getting the customer's attention in the moment to helping them take a small action—rehanging their towel.

Delivery

If you've stayed in a hotel over the last couple of years, you will have seen notices in hotel bathrooms that act as nudges, encouraging guests to do their bit for the environment by reusing their towels. Researchers studied which of the four messages trialled in their study were most effective. Two of the messages, written on small signs placed in the bathroom, encouraged guests to partner with the hotel to save energy or to help protect the environment. The other two notices stated firstly that 75 percent of hotel guests reuse their towels and more specifically that 75 percent of guests who stayed in that very room reused their towels.

Outcome

All of the notices had some positive effect in changing behaviour. The most effective message was found to be one that read, 'Over 75% of the guests who stay in this room decide to reuse their towels a second day. Please hang your towels if you also want to reuse your towels tomorrow.'

The messages that urged guests to help the hotel save energy or protect the environment were significantly less effective than messages pointing to social norms. In other words, we want to conform with what our peers are doing. We want to fit in and to belong. That deep-seated need can be tapped to change behaviour.

HOW LUNE CROISSANTERIE BUILT A CULT FOLLOWING

You can buy an ordinary croissant in a supermarket or corner bakery anywhere in the world. Kate Reid wanted to make the perfect Australian croissant—one that people would cross town for.

Drivers

Kate Reid's childhood dream was to work in Formula One racing. She excelled in maths and science at school, and went on to spend five years studying engineering at university. Reid did eventually land her dream job in Europe, but the dream of working in the racing industry didn't match the reality. Reid began to question whether she had chosen the right career path. Back home in Australia and considering her options, she couldn't stop thinking about doing something with baking. Reid got a job serving behind the counter in a local bakery, but soon realised that she really wanted to be making the products.

One morning she was leafing through a book about Parisienne patisseries when she came across a picture of perfect *pain au chocolat*. Reid shut the book, walked up the street and booked herself on a flight to Paris. Once there, she talked her way into an apprenticeship with the renowned baker Christophe Vasseur, who ran Du Pain et des Idées, where the pastries in the book she'd read back home had been baked.

When Reid returned to Melbourne, she realised she couldn't reproduce the French croissants because Australian ingredients were different. So, she started from scratch, bringing everything she had learned in the Paris bakery and combining it with the rigour of science and maths. Her croissants take three days to make. Kate and her brother Cameron opened their hole-in-the-wall bakery, Lune Croissanterie, in a bayside suburb of Melbourne in 2012. Their intention was to build a trusted reputation in the local neighbourhood and to market the business by word of mouth.

Delivery

Lune's story starts with Reid perfecting her craft. She made a croissant worth talking about. Lune initially only opened three, then four days a week and closed when the pastries were sold. Some days they were sold out before midday. The limited opening hours created scarcity. Opening fewer days meant that the Reid's could manage their workload, hand-rolling pastries to their own exacting standards. This also had the happy side effect of creating lines out the door and around the block on the days they were open. Good news travelled fast and soon people from other suburbs were coming to line up. Lune was so successful that they had to move to bigger premises. The centrepiece of the new purpose-built bakery is a climate-controlled glass room where people can watch the labour of love and precision as the Reid's hand-roll croissants. Beyond the quality of their product, the packaging, pricing, location and limited opening hours were tactical decisions that helped Lune to differentiate their business.

Outcome

Kate Reid set out to make the kind of product that people didn't need to be persuaded to try more than once—a croissant so good they'd pay more and be willing to wait in line for it. The quality of her product and the rhythm and the ritual of her customer's week helped Lune to build brand loyalty with customers. The Reid's have created an incredibly successful business through word of mouth. The icing on the cake? Lune was featured in an article in the *New York Times* in 2016, under this headline, 'The Best Croissants in the World?'

HOW ODDBOX MADE WONKY FRUIT AND VEGETABLES A HIT

Each year 1.3 billion tonnes of food produced is wasted. Over 10 million tonnes (worth an estimated 17 billion pounds) is wasted just in the UK. Three million tonnes are wasted before it even leaves the farm—enough food to feed 20,000 people for a year. Oddbox is a UK based fruit and vegetable delivery service. The company wants to tackle food waste, starting with 5 percent of the on-farm food waste in the UK.

Drivers

A huge percentage of the fruit and vegetables grown by farmers globally is wasted because it doesn't meet supermarket's strict aesthetic standards. Supermarket customers reject fresh produce that doesn't fit with their perception of what a perfect piece of fruit or veg should look like. Farmers can't sell this produce to supermarkets, so tonnes of it is wasted every year. To help solve this problem, Oddbox wanted to partner with growers to salvage their perfectly good, fresh but misshapen produce. The company needed to change the prospective customer's perception about fresh produce perfection. Oddbox's strategy depended on their message hitting home with customers who shared their values and worldview.

Delivery

Oddbox began offering delivery of a fruit and veg box that was full only of misshapen fruit and vegetables at a price point that's 30 percent less than companies delivering conventional 'perfect' fruit and veg boxes. Part of their storytelling strategy is reduced pricing. But the message the company leads with is waste reduction. They are educating customers about the scale of the problem. If you're the kind of person who cares about the environment, food waste and poverty, then it's likely that supporting Oddbox will align with your values and reinforce the story you tell yourself about how you are doing your bit. The company's brand name calls out their key differentiator and positions them in a market of one.

Outcome

Oddbox experienced sales growth of 650 percent between April 2017 and 2018. At the time of writing, the company has 2,500 people on its waiting list to become customers. Oddbox has plans to expand its delivery and storage capabilities to meet demand.

What we see from these stories is that the brands that succeeded in telling the right story spent the majority of their time understanding the change they wanted to create and the impact they wanted to have. They developed superior products and understood who it was for, before they began to tell the story to those prospective customers. They didn't focus only on how they could get the customer to act. They considered the role the company or organisation had to play as they helped to change people's minds and win their hearts.

CONCLUSION

"Progress is impossible without change, and those who cannot change their minds cannot change anything."

—GEORGE BERNARD SHAW

SOMETHING TO BELIEVE IN

On a beautiful autumn day in 1951, Ellen Slevin packed a small bag for a journey she'd made many times over the past fifteen years. There was no time to waste. As the mother of 10 children, Ellen knew better than most that a baby ready to be born waited for no woman, or man for that matter. She should get to the Coombe hospital sooner rather

✳

Persuasion does not have to be a selfish act. It can be how we choose to change things for the better.

✳

than later. With any luck she'd be back before dark—tomorrow at the latest.

Ellen never did come home. She died in childbirth. There were complications during the delivery—a pulmonary embolism, septicaemia. In Ireland back then it wasn't uncommon for a mother to die during a difficult birth. The baby, her eighth son and eleventh child survived. Ellen was 38 when she died. My father, her second son was 12 at the time.

The Offences Against the Person Act passed in Ireland in 1861 made 'procuring' or assisting in the procurement of a miscarriage a crime punishable by life imprisonment. Abortion was illegal in Ireland. In 1983 a referendum to amend the constitution was passed. Here's what it said:

'The State acknowledges the right to life of the unborn and, with due regard to the equal right to life of the mother, guarantees in its laws to respect, and, as far as practicable, by its laws to defend and vindicate that right.'

Because Ireland was and still is a predominantly Catholic country, contraception or contraceptive advice was not available to couples through most of the twentieth century. It was not unusual for women in the mid-1900s to give birth to 10 or more children. A pregnancy occurring out of wedlock brought deep shame. Many young unmarried women were cast out of their communities when they became pregnant. Many concealed unwanted pregnancies and travelled to England to get abortions or to have their babies adopted. Victims of rape and women who were terminally ill or carrying children with disabilities found it impossible to get the help and support they needed. Terrible stories of newborns abandoned or dumped or found in shallow graves changed nothing. Access to abortion services or counselling was denied for decades.

It wasn't until 1992, in the wake of Case X—that of a 14-year-old rape victim whose pregnancy caused her to become suicidal—that it became legal for women to travel outside Ireland to have a pregnancy terminated if it was deemed that their life was at risk (including by suicide). By 1995 doctors, counsellors and advisory services were allowed to provide information about abortion outside the State. Over the years several stories about women suffering health risks and psychological trauma because of the law came to light. In the summer of 2014, the UN Human Rights Committee (UNHC) criticised Ireland's abortion laws, calling on its government to change the constitution and legislation. In 2017 the UNHC stated that the "prohibition of abortion in Ireland targets women, by virtue of being women, and places them in a particular situation of vulnerability, which discriminates against them in relation to men."

But those calls were made too late to save the life of Savita Halappanavar. Her story became the tipping point that would eventually give Irish women more control over their reproductive rights, and enable the Irish medical profession to prioritise the wellbeing of pregnant women as well as the right to life of the unborn children.

Generations of women had fought to overturn the law that protected the right of the child to life which had been written into the country's constitution since 1983, with little success. Data about the potential

Trust is fast becoming our scarcest and most valuable resource.

harm to women, and statistics about the health risks and emotional cost and the trauma experienced often by teenage women, had changed nothing. In the end, it was Savita's story that changed everything.

Savita Halappanavar was 31 years old, and 17 weeks pregnant with her first child. Accompanied by her husband Praveen, she presented with low back pain at University Hospital Galway on the morning of Sunday 21st October 2012. The couple were reassured and sent home, but they returned later that afternoon. Savita was distressed and in a lot of pain. The midwife thought she was having a miscarriage and called the doctor. The inevitable loss of the pregnancy was confirmed, but since a foetal heartbeat could still be detected, Savita was admitted to allow events to take their natural course. Over the next two days, Savita's symptoms worsened; she was vomiting and bleeding and her water broke. On Tuesday, she and her husband requested medication to induce the inevitable miscarriage. Their request was refused. Under Irish law, if the mother's life was not at risk, doctors couldn't provide such medication while there was a foetal heartbeat. By Wednesday morning, Savita was transferred to theatre to have a central line inserted to treat what was now diagnosed as septic shock. She finally miscarried in theatre. But her condition worsened and she was transferred to ICU and put on a ventilator. Savita died in the small hours of Sunday morning, a week after she went to the hospital. It was shown later that doctors had missed signs that Savita's life was in danger.

When the news story about Savita's death broke, it was met by a wave of public anger. The nation was appalled. Questions about how such a thing could happen in 21st-century Ireland were raised and debated. Savita's story was headline news for months. It was also the catalyst for the #neveragain movement that took hold. 'She had a heartbeat, too' was the rallying cry.

The Protection of Life During Pregnancy Act 2013 was passed as a result of Savita's death. And then in May 2018, a referendum was held to repeal the Eighth Amendment to the Constitution, to allow Parliament to legislate on abortion. Sixty-six percent of Irish voters voted Yes to repealing the Eighth Amendment. Back in Savita's native India, her parents expressed their gratitude to the people of Ireland and requested that the new law to grant women reproductive rights be named Savita's Law.

This change took decades. In the end, it wasn't the statistics about the numbers of deaths or women travelling to the UK to terminate unwanted pregnancies that persuaded the majority of people that something had to change. It was one woman's story.

Persuasion has become a dirty word. Since the days when the admen of Madison Avenue took on the job of convincing men and women that smoking cigarettes was good for them, the marketing industry and the thousands of people who work in it have been getting a bad rap. Many people in sales and marketing roles today are secretly ashamed or disquieted to belong to the profession they're in. Marketing is often associated with tricking people into buying things they don't need and making decisions they will later regret. The word conjures up images of travelling snake oil salesmen and people with the privilege of

✳

There is no trust without stories we can believe in.

access to education and information preying on the gullible or the vulnerable. More recently, marketing has been connected with stories about organisations built to mine personal data with the sole and express purpose of planting ideas, supported by fake data and fake news in the minds of people who later regret voting for something they didn't fully understand. No wonder it's getting hard to find people who are proud to call themselves marketers.

While it's important to call out unscrupulous people and organisations—the Bernard Madoffs and Cambridge Analytica's of the world who abuse knowledge, status and power to deceive, defraud and destroy people's trust and lives—it's equally important to point out that marketing and storytelling have been incredible forces for positive change in our world. The global movements that raise our consciousness, nudging us towards the kind of future we want to see—microlending, gay rights, fair trade, voting rights for women and B Corporations, to name a few—would not have succeeded without great storytellers and storytelling that moved people. Persuasion does not have to be a selfish act. It can be how we choose to change things for the better.

In a world of infinite choices, decision-making is inevitable. Our job as ethical changemakers is to speak truth to people we care about serving and to help them to make the most informed and best decisions for them. To do that we must flip what we've been conditioned to believe about persuasion on its head.

What if, instead of taking impatient shortcuts in an attempt to get more people to act, we spent time earning the trust of the people we want to matter to? What if every story we told came from a place of deep conviction and empathy with the people whose lives we are hoping to influence for the better? How would our stories change too?

As our populations have become more mobile and our technology has enabled connection across geographical boundaries, our neighbourhoods have disintegrated, our tribes diversified. For a while we had begun to treat trust as an optional extra. We're coming to realise that when you can't look someone in the eye, trust is not only essential—trust is everything.

Trust is fast becoming our scarcest and most valuable resource.

There is no trust without stories we can believe in. Without trust there is no change. It's only by telling stories that forge trust that we can imagine our collective future together on this planet, or indeed on any other. Resources and science can give us the wherewithal—the dollars, data and discoveries that might one day propel us forward—but without the will to harness them, we stand still. Without creativity and innovation, knowledge and money are worthless. We must have the humanity and the heart to harness them.

Every step towards positive change starts with an act of persuasion, the ability to influence someone to join or belong. You can't change people without first engaging with their humanity. Stories are a compass for the heart. They move us to act, to create a better future we cannot yet see. From the Viking voyages across uncharted waters to unconquered territories, to the excavation of historical artefacts from the ground in Wood Quay, it's always been the will of the

✳

*Stories are
a compass for
the heart.*

✳

people, not the machinery that changed everything. Automation and digitisation haven't altered that fact. Whether our ideas, innovations, communities and societies survive and thrive is still dependent on our ability to unite and work towards shared goals. Equality, justice, fairness, sustainability, creativity, innovation and our collective prosperity rely on us trusting enough to come together.

I started this book by inviting you to think about why we need stories. I want to end it by asking you to think about the places where you use those stories, and about the change you're trying to create—the skin you want to get under, the hearts you want to touch, the lives you want to make better. Any endeavour is about creating a future you want to see. An abundant society can't be created with a narrative of scarcity.

The gap between what we can imagine and our ability to do it is shrinking. But simply having the ways and means is not enough to change things. One person with unlimited resources changes nothing. A community of committed people with a shared goal and limited resources can change everything. The right story isn't the point. The right change, at the right time, for the right people and the right reason is the point. Arriving shouldn't be the only thing we prioritise. When you do finally get to where you were headed, you realise that change wasn't as important as bringing people with you on the journey. What binds us on our journey together was, is still and always will be, the story of where we hope to go next. When we are united by that story and our shared humanity, rather than separated by our otherness, we can change anything and everything for the better. Together.

REFERENCES

INTRODUCTION

'The real difference between chimpanzees and us' — Yuval Noah Harari, 'Dreaming the World', YNHarari.com. http://www.ynharari.com/topic/power-and-imagination/

'Layer upon layer of urban living' — Linzi Simpson, 'Heritage Outrage: Wood Quay', *History Ireland*, Vol. 22 No. 2. https://www.historyireland.com/volume-22/heritage-outrage-wood-quay/

Carly Hilts, 'Wood Quay: Revealing the Heart of Viking Dublin', *Current Archaeology* 328. https://www.archaeology.co.uk/articles/features/wood-quay-revealing-the-heart-of-viking-dublin.htm

'Drowned in a sea of steel and cement', 1980, archived newscast, RTE.ie. https://www.rte.ie/archives/2015/0629/711292-work-on-second-ten-storey-tower-on-wood-quay/

Kate Hickey, 'The truth about High King of Ireland Brian Boru on the anniversary of his death', IrishCentral.com, 23 April 2017. https://www.irishcentral.com/roots/history/brian-boru-battle-of-clontarf

What's the point of stories?

'Human brain – Neuroscience – Cognitive Science' BasicKnowledge101.com. http://www.basicknowledge101.com/subjects/brain.html

'Oxytocin (the neurochemical responsible for empathy and narrative transportation) is synthesized' — Paul J. Zak, PhD., 'Why Inspiring Stories Make Us React: The Neuroscience of Narrative', *Cerebrum*, Vol. 2015 2. https://www.ncbi.nlm.nih.gov/pmc/articles/PMC4445577/

'Stories that are personal and emotionally compelling' — Paul J. Zak, PhD., 'How Stories Change the Brain', *Greater Good Magazine*, 17 December 2013. https://greatergood.berkeley.edu/article/item/how_stories_change_brain

Paul J. Zak, Robert Kurzban, & William T. Matzner, 'The Neurobiology of Trust', *Annals of the New York Academy of Sciences*, Vol. 1032 No. 1. The neurobiology of trust. Zak PJ, Kurzban R, Matzner WT Ann N Y Acad Sci. 2004 Dec; 1032():224-7

WHAT IS THE RIGHT STORY?

Change is a human act

B. J. Fogg, 'B. J. Fogg's Behavior Model', BehaviorModel. org. http://www.behaviormodel.org/

Robert Cialdini, PhD., 'Principles of Persuasion', InfluenceAtWork.com. https://www.influenceatwork.com/ principles-of-persuasion/

Geoffrey A. Moore, *Crossing the Chasm: Marketing and Selling Disruptive Products to Mainstream Customers*, 3ed. New York: HarperCollins, 2014.

The process of persuasion

Cialdini, 'Principles of Persuasion'.

Robert Cialdini, PhD., 'Science of Persuasion', video presentation. https://www.youtube.com/ watch?v=cFdCzN7RYbw

Fogg, 'B. J. Fogg's Behavior Model'.

Abhijit Vinayak Banerjee, Esther Duflo, Rachel Glennerster, & Dhruva Kothari, 'Improving Immunization Coverage in Rural India: A Clustered Randomized Controlled Evaluation of Immunization Campaigns with and without Incentives', *BMJ* 2010;340;c2220.

Dina Grossman, 'Incentives for Immunization', *J-PAL Policy Briefcase*. Cambridge, MA: Abdul Latif Jameel Poverty Action Lab, 2011.

The commercialisation of persuasion

'History of Advertising', Wikipedia.org. https:// en.wikipedia.org/wiki/History_of_advertising

Al Ries & Jack Trout, *Positioning: The Battle for Your Mind*. New York: McGraw-Hill Professional, 2011.

Making change happen

Guy Raz, 'How I Built This', interview transcript, NPR. org,12 February 2018. https://www.npr.org/templates/ transcript/transcript.php?storyId=584331881

Paul Sandle, 'Dyson posts $1.1 bln profit driven by Asian demand for its tech', Reuters.com, 28 February 2018. https:// www.reuters.com/article/britain-dyson-results/dyson-posts-1-1-bln-profit-driven-by-asian-demand-for-its-tech-idUSL8N1QI9D8

Priming and Timing

'No story lives' — J. K. Rowling speaking at Trafalgar Square. Stuart Kemp, 'J. K. Rowling, Emma Watson in tears at *Harry Potter* premiere', HollywoodReporter.com, 8 July 2011. https://www.hollywoodreporter.com/news/jk-rowling-emma-watson-potter-208901

The Change journey

Malcolm Gladwell, *The Tipping Point: How Little Things Can Make a Big Difference.* New York: Little, Brown & Company 2011.

Purposeful Storytelling

'Golden Gate Bridge', Wikipedia.org. https://en.wikipedia.org/wiki/Golden_Gate_Bridge
'Toll Rates & Traffic Operations', GoldenGateBridge.org. http://goldengatebridge.org/tolls_traffic/

Katy Steinmetz, 'Officials consider Golden Gate Bridge toll for pedestrians', Time.com, 24 October 2014. http://time.com/3535150/officials-consider-golden-gate-bridge-toll-for-pedestrians/

Christina Bonnington, 'Tourists ruined the Golden Gate Bridge', TheBoldItalic.com, 3 July 2017. https://thebolditalic.com/tourists-ruined-the-golden-gate-bridge-d2d6868ffb45

THE STORY COMPASS

Story Drivers

'Why Water?', CharityWater.org. https://www.charitywater.org/global-water-crisis

Ken Stern, With Charity for All: Why Charities Are Failing and a Better Way to Give. New York: Knopf Doubleday 2013. https://www.penguinrandomhouse.com/books/210087/with-charity-for-all-by-ken-stern/9780307743817/

Story Delivery

'Her Royal Highness the Duchess of Sussex Carries Strathberry in Dublin, Ireland', Strathberry.com, 10 July 2018. Strathberry.com https://www.strathberry.com/blogs/house-of-strathberry/her-royal-highness-the-duchess-of-sussex-carries-strathberry-in-dublin-ireland

Conviction and Courage

Clark Mindock, 'Taking a knee: Why are NFL players protesting and when did they start to kneel?', The Independent, 4 September 2018. https://www.independent.co.uk/news/world/americas/us-politics/taking-a-knee-national-anthem-nfl-trump-why-meaning-origins-racism-us-colin-kaepernick-a8521741.html

Adam Stites, 'Everything you need to know about NFL protests during the national anthem', SBNation.com, 19 October 2017. https://www.sbnation.com/2017/9/29/16380080/donald-trump-nfl-colin-kaepernick-protests-national-anthem

Scott Galloway, 'Best and worst brand moves of 2018', Gartner L2, 7 September 2018. https://www.l2inc.com/daily-insights/no-mercy-no-malice/best-and-worst-brand-moves-of-2018

Scott Galloway, 'The Gangster Marketing Move of 2018', Youtube.com, 5 September 2018. https://youtu.be/qLXzPDteFks

GOING NARROW AND DEEP

Iceland

Emma Young, 'Iceland knows how to stop teen substance abuse but the rest of the world isn't listening', Mosaic, 17 January 2017. https://mosaicscience.com/story/iceland-prevent-teen-substance-abuse/

Mecca Cosmetica

'The idea was to bring' — Jo-Anne Hui-Miller, 'From the source: Jo Horgan, Mecca Cosmetica', Inside Retail Australia, 13 October 2017. https://www.insideretail.com.au/news/from-the-source-jo-horgan-mecca-cosmetica-201710

Airbnb

'Airbnb', GrowthHackers.com. https://growthhackers.com/growth-studies/airbnb

Lululemon

Guy Raz, 'How I Built This', interview transcript, NPR.org, 18 June 2018. https://www.npr.org/templates/transcript/transcript.php?storyId=620113439

'Encouraging participation in sports and growing penchant for fitness drive demand for sports and fitness clothing', Global Industry Analysts, Inc., April 2018. https://www.strategyr.com/MarketResearch/Sports_and_Fitness_Clothing_Market_Trends.asp

Lindsey Rupp & Anders Melin, 'Lululemon founder sells chunk of stake to fund other ventures', Bloomberg.com, 15 February 2018. https://www.bloomberg.com/news/articles/2018-02-15/lululemon-founder-sells-chunk-of-stake-to-fund-other-ventures

Lindsey Rupp, 'Lululemon surges the most in 10 months after online sales boom', Bloomberg.com, 27 March 2018. https://www.bloomberg.com/news/articles/2018-03-27/lululemon-surges-after-growth-quells-fears-about-empty-ceo-suite

'lululemon athletica', eMarketer Retail, 2018. https://retail-index.emarketer.com/company/5374f24c4d4afd2bb44465b9/lululemon-athletica/

'Ambassadors', Lululemon.com. https://shop.lululemon.com/ambassadors/_/N-1z141e2?mnid=mn;en-CA-JSON;community;ambassadors

'Yoga – statistics and facts', Statista.com, 2018. https://www.statista.com/topics/3229/yoga/

Yashaswini Swamynathan, 'Lululemon hits record high on revamped stores', Reuters.com, 1 June 2018. https://www.reuters.com/article/us-lululemon-stocks/lululemon-hits-record-high-on-revamped-stores-idUSKCN1IX4LD

Hotel towels

Lucy Siegle, 'Ethical living: Is it worth reusing our hotel towels?', The Guardian, 23 September 2012. https://www.theguardian.com/environment/2012/sep/23/lucy-siegle-ethical-living-hotel-towels

'The research behind guest behavior: Example – towel reuse', CERT, 2011. https://www.cleanenergyresourceteams.org/files/ResearchBehindGuestBehavior_TowelReuse_1-24-11.pdf

Rachel Nuwer, 'Reusing hotel towels actually does make a difference', Smithsonian.com, 25 February 2014. https://www.smithsonianmag.com/smart-news/reusing-hotel-towels-actually-does-make-difference-180949890/

Lune Croissanterie

Dana McCauley, "How Kate Reid invented the 'world's best croissant' through reverse engineering", News.com. au, 7 September 2017. https://www.news.com.au/finance/ business/other-industries/how-kate-reid-invented-the- worlds-best-croissant-through-reverse-engineering/news-st ory/22b124b72a372d768030032941852345

Oliver Strand, 'Is the world's best croissant made in Australia?', New York Times Magazine, 11 April 2016. https://www.nytimes.com/2016/04/11/t-magazine/food/ lune-croissanterie-melbourne-croissants.html

Oddbox

'Why We Do It', Oddbox.co.uk. https://www.oddbox. co.uk/why/

Madelyn Newton, 'Oddbox launches crowdfunding campaign to fuel wonky veg revolution', BusinessGreen. com, 10 July 2018. https://www.businessgreen.com/bg/ news/3035579/oddbox-launches-crowdfunding-campaign- to-fuel-wonky-veg-revolution

CONCLUSION

'Progress is impossible without change' — George Bernard Shaw, *Everybody's Political What's What?* London: Constable Limited 1944.

Something to believe in

'The Attorney General (Plaintiff) v. X. and Others (Defendant)', Supreme Court of Ireland Decisions, 5 March 1992. http://www.bailii.org/ie/cases/IESC/1992/1.html

'History of Abortion in Ireland', Irish Family Planning Association. https://www.ifpa.ie/advocacy/abortion-in-ireland-legal-timeline/

Sinead O'Carroll, 'Savita Halappanavar: Her tragic death and how she became part of Ireland's abortion debate', TheJournal.ie, 29 April 2018. http://www.thejournal.ie/eighth-amendment-4-3977441-Apr2018/

Kitty Holland & Paul Cullen, 'Woman 'denied a termination' dies in hospital', The Irish Times, 14 November 2012. https://www.irishtimes.com/news/woman-denied-a-termination-dies-in-hospital-1.551412

Harriet Sherwood & Lisa O'Carroll, 'Yes campaigners want Irish abortion legislation to be 'Savita's law', The Guardian, 27 May 2018. https://www.theguardian.com/world/2018/may/27/ireland-abortion-law-named-after-savita-halappanavar

ACKNOWLEDGEMENTS

Any act of change takes a village and so does any act of creation. Even independent artists aren't really working alone. We are shaped by the people who touch us and our work and by those our work touches. These are the people who have shaped me and this book.

Thank you for buying and reading this book. It's a privilege to write for and share ideas with you. One I don't take for granted.

Thank you:

Seth Godin for inspiring me and thousands of others to show up and decide to change tiny corners of the world. Reese Spykerman for creating design that moves people and inspiring me to do better work.

Kelly Exeter for doing the tedious work of interior layout, but more, for caring about readers and books in equal measure. Catherine Oliver for pointing out the holes in early drafts. Nena Rawdah for patiently working with me to make this a better book and Leanne Wickham for spotting the tiny details that matter. Chris Finnegan, Michael Brockie and Josh Anthony, the team a WPCopilot, whose expertise and kind hearts make it easier for me to tell the right story online. Trent Innes, Rod Moynihan, Lynda Talintyre, and Sarah Reed for inviting me to share the work on storytelling, that was the genesis of this book, with the Xero and Zendesk communities. Mark Dyck for wholeheartedly helping me to create the future we want to see for business owners. Members of *the* Right Company community and readers of my blog for giving me a reason to be curious, notice and write. And Moyez, Adam, Kieran and Matthew for reminding me why any and all of this matters.

ABOUT THE AUTHOR

Bernadette Jiwa was born in Dublin, the storytelling capital of the world, and is now lucky enough to call Melbourne Australia, the world's most liveable city, home.

Bernadette is a recognised global authority on strategic storytelling. Named by Smart Company as one of the Top Business Thinkers of 2018, she is the author of several bestselling books on marketing and brand storytelling and founder of the Right Company business community.

Her popular blog (TheStoryofTelling.com/blog) was voted Best Australian Business Blog in 2012 and was featured three times in Smart Company's Best Australian Business Blog list, topping it in 2016.

Seth Godin listed it as one of the few business blogs he reads.

Bernadette advises, consults and speaks with entrepreneurs and business leaders, from start-ups to *Fortune* 500 companies, who want to do work they're proud of and create the future they want to see. Her work takes her from Melbourne to New York (and everywhere in between).

thestoryoftelling.com

35582010R00106

Made in the USA
Middletown, DE
07 February 2019